KNOW YOUR FOOD

GLUTEN

KNOW YOUR FOOD

KNOW YOUR FOOD

Gluten

MICHAEL CENTORE

MASON CREST

Mason Crest
450 Parkway Drive, Suite D
Broomall, PA 19008
www.masoncrest.com

MTM Publishing, Inc.
435 West 23rd Street, #8C
New York, NY 10011
www.mtmpublishing.com

President: Valerie Tomaselli
Vice President, Book Development: Hilary Poole
Designer: Annemarie Redmond
Copyeditor: Peter Jaskowiak
Editorial Assistant: Leigh Eron

Series ISBN: 978-1-4222-3733-5
Hardback ISBN: 978-1-4222-3739-7
E-Book ISBN: 978-1-4222-8046-1

Library of Congress Cataloging-in-Publication Data
Names: Centore, Michael, 1980-author.
Title: Gluten / by Michael Centore.
Description: Broomall, PA: Mason Crest, [2018] | Series: Know your food | Audience: Ages 12+. |
   Audience: Grades 7 to 8. | Includes bibliographical references and index.
Identifiers: LCCN 2016053142 (print) | LCCN 2017016845 (ebook) | ISBN 9781422280461 (ebook) |
   ISBN 9781422237397 (hardback: alk. paper)
Subjects: LCSH: Gluten—Juvenile literature. | Gluten—Health aspects—Juvenile literature. | Celiac
   disease—Juvenile literature. | Gluten-free diet—Juvenile literature.
Classification: LCC QK898.G49 (ebook) | LCC QK898.G49 C46 2017 (print) | DDC
   613.2/82—dc23
LC record available at https://lccn.loc.gov/2016053142

Printed and bound in the United States of America.

First printing
9 8 7 6 5 4 3 2 1

TABLE OF CONTENTS

Key Icons to Look for:

Words to Understand: These words with their easy-to-understand definitions will increase the reader's understanding of the text, while building vocabulary skills.

Sidebars: This boxed material within the main text allows readers to build knowledge, gain insights, explore possibilities, and broaden their perspectives by weaving together additional information to provide realistic and holistic perspectives.

Educational Videos: Readers can view videos by scanning our QR codes, which will provide them with additional educational content to supplement the text. Examples include news coverage, moments in history, speeches, iconic sports moments, and much more.

Text-Dependent Questions: These questions send the reader back to the text for more careful attention to the evidence presented there.

Research Projects: Readers are pointed toward areas of further inquiry connected to each chapter. Suggestions are provided for projects that encourage deeper research and analysis.

Series Glossary of Key Terms: This back-of-the-book glossary contains terminology used throughout the series. Words found here increase the reader's ability to read and comprehend higher-level books and articles in this field.

SERIES INTRODUCTION

In the early 19th century, a book was published in France called *Physiologie du goût* (*The Physiology of Taste*), and since that time, it has never gone out of print. Its author was Jean Anthelme Brillat-Savarin. Brillat-Savarin is still considered to be one of the great food writers, and he was, to use our current lingo, arguably the first "foodie." Among other pearls, *Physiologie du goût* gave us one of the quintessential aphorisms about dining: "Tell me what you eat, and I will tell you what you are."

This concept was introduced to Americans in the 20th century by a nutritionist named Victor Lindlahr, who wrote simply, "You are what you eat." Lindlahr interpreted the saying literally: if you eat healthy food, he argued, you will become a healthy person.

But Brillat-Savarin likely had something a bit more metaphorical in mind. His work suggested that the dishes we create and consume have not only nutritional implications, but ethical, philosophical, and even political implications, too.

To be clear, Brillat-Savarin had a great deal to say on the importance of nutrition. In his writings he advised people to limit their intake of "floury and starchy substances," and for that reason he is sometimes considered to be the inventor of the low-carb diet. But Brillat-Savarin also took the idea of dining extremely seriously. He was devoted to the notion of pleasure in eating and was a fierce advocate of the importance of being a good host. In fact, he went so far as to say that anyone who doesn't make an effort to feed his guests "does not deserve to have friends." Brillat-Savarin also understood that food was at once deeply personal and extremely social. "Cooking is one of the oldest arts," he wrote, "and one that has rendered us the most important service in civic life."

Modern diners and cooks still grapple with the many implications of Brillat-Savarin's most famous statement. Certainly on a nutritional level, we understand that a diet that's low in fat and high in whole grains is a key to healthy living. This is no minor issue. Unless our current course is reversed, today's "obesity epidemic" is poised to significantly reduce the life spans of future generations.

Meanwhile, we are becoming increasingly aware of how the decisions we make at supermarkets can ripple outward, impacting our neighborhoods, nations, and the earth as a whole. Increasing numbers of us are demanding organically produced foods and ethically sourced ingredients. Some shoppers reject products that contain artificial ingredients like trans fats or high-fructose corn syrup. Some adopt gluten-free or vegan diets, while others "go Paleo" in the hopes of returning to a more "natural" way of eating. A simple trip to the supermarket can begin to feel like a personality test—the implicit question is not only "what does a *healthy* person eat?," but also "what does a *good* person eat?"

The Know Your Food series introduces students to these complex issues by looking at the various components that make up our meals: carbohydrates, fats, proteins, vitamins, and so on. Each volume focuses on one component and explains its function in our bodies, how it gets into food, how it changes when cooked, and what happens when we consume too much or too little. The volumes also look at food production—for example, how did the food dye called Red No. 2 end up in our food, and why was it taken out? What are genetically modified organisms, and are they safe or not? Along the way, the volumes also explore different diets, such as low-carb, low-fat, vegetarian, and gluten-free, going beyond the hype to examine their potential benefits and possible downsides.

Each chapter features definitions of key terms for that specific section, while a Series Glossary at the back provides an overview of words that are most important to the set overall. Chapters have Text-Dependent Questions at the end, to help students assess their comprehension of the most important material, as well as suggested Research Projects that will help them continue their exploration. Last but not least, QR codes accompany each chapter; students with cell phones or tablets can scan these codes for videos that will help bring the topics to life. (Those without devices can access the videos via an Internet browser; the addresses are included at the end of the Further Reading list.)

In the spirit of Brillat-Savarin, the volumes in this set look beyond nutrition to also consider various historical, political, and ethical aspects of food. Whether it's the key role that sugar played in the slave trade, the implications of industrial meat production in the fight against climate change, or the short-sighted political decisions that resulted in the water catastrophe in Flint, Michigan, the Know Your Food series introduces students to the ways in which a meal can be, in a real sense, much more than just a meal.

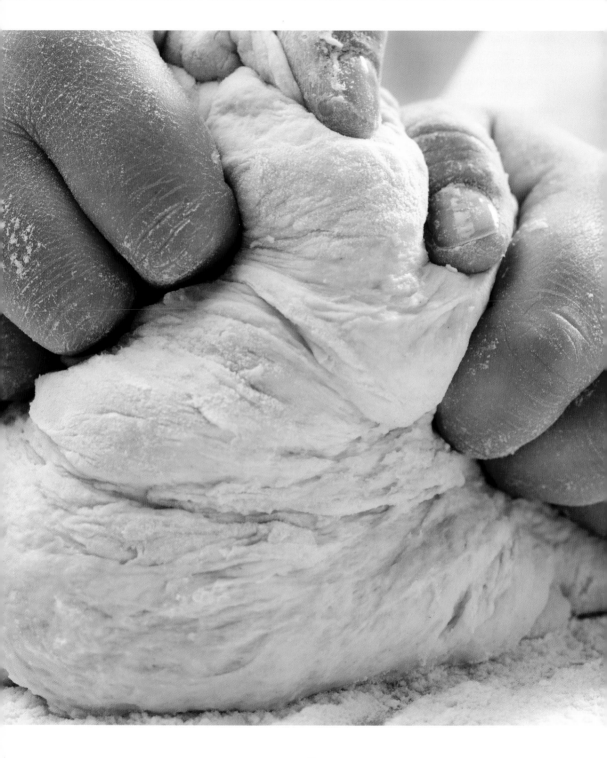

WHAT IS GLUTEN?

 ## WORDS TO UNDERSTAND

carbohydrates: organic compounds containing carbon, hydrogen, and oxygen (like sugars and starches) that can be broken down to produce energy in plants and animals.

crossbreeding: combining different species or varieties of plants or animals into a new organism.

endosperm: a tissue produced in the seeds of flowering plants to provide nutrition to the embryo.

gliadin: along with glutenin, one of the two storage proteins that make up gluten.

glutelin: a type of protein found in many grass-related grains that can be dissolved in certain acids or bases.

glutenin: along with gliadin, one of the two storage proteins that make up gluten.

lipid: a type of fatty acid such as oil or wax.

prolamin: a type of protein found in many grass-related grains that can be dissolved in some alcohol solutions.

O n the popular late-night television show *Jimmy Kimmel Live*, a field reporter asked four Los Angeles residents whether they kept a gluten-free diet. All four responded yes. The reporter pressed on with the question, asking, "What is gluten?" Answers ranged from "a flour derivative" to "a part of the wheat" to a simple "I don't know." Not one of the interviewees understood exactly what they were so studiously avoiding.

The lesson? Gluten may be all over the news, with a glut of gluten-free cookbooks sagging the shelves of bookstores and gluten-free options popping up on restaurant menus, but there is still a lot of misinformation (and just plain confusion) about this humble protein. Derided as a "poison" or "silent killer" by one person and brushed aside as harmless by the next, gluten remains one of the most controversial—and widely consumed—food products on earth. Understanding gluten's potential benefits and adverse effects can help you make educated choices about its place in your diet. It starts by answering the question that those *Kimmel* subjects couldn't: What is it?

EDUCATIONAL VIDEO

WHAT IS GLUTEN?

Scan this code to see a video that explains more about gluten.

BUILDING UP GLUTEN

The simplest definition is that gluten is a protein. Proteins are large molecules found in the cells of all living organisms. They are crucial to all aspects of physical growth and development, and they also participate in many cellular functions, from setting chemical reactions in motion to transporting water and minerals into and out of the cell. Some proteins are storage proteins, meaning that they store reserves of amino acids (the building blocks of protein) for the future maintenance and growth of the organism.

Proteins in wheat and other cereal grains are classified into four groups:

1. albumins, which can be dissolved in water;
2. globulins, which can be dissolved in salt solutions;
3. prolamins, which can be dissolved in some alcohol solutions; and

4. glutelins, which can be dissolved in certain acids or bases.

The proteins that make up gluten are the last two: prolamins and glutelins. The glutelin protein in wheat is called glutenin, and the prolamin protein is called gliadin. Both glutenin and gliadin are storage proteins. They are found in the wheat's endosperm, where they retain nutrients used to help feed the plant's embryo—the young, developing plant within the seed, also called the wheat germ.

Gluten is formed when wheat flour is mixed with water. As the glutenin and gliadin proteins are hydrated, they begin to form chemical bonds called cross-links. The more the flour and water is mixed, the more the glutenin and gliadin rearrange and reshape themselves to form more cross-links. Little by little, as the dough is kneaded by hand or machine, the proteins form "networks" of gluten. Air trapped within the dough helps

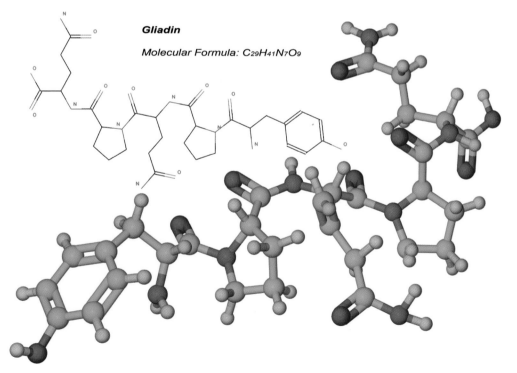

Gliadin

Molecular Formula: $C_{29}H_{41}N_7O_9$

The chemical structure of gliadin, one of two major protein components of gluten.

11

The properties of gluten make it possible for chefs to stretch and knead their dough; this is often an amusing part of pizza making.

strengthen the protein bonds. Soon the networks combine into sheet-like structures, almost as if the "threads" of the proteins are being "woven" into pieces of fabric.

Gluten is a strong, elastic substance that gives dough its stretchy quality and bread and other baked goods their chewy texture. It is no wonder that *gluten* in Latin means "glue": it helps the dough cohere and keep its shape, even when it is tugged or pulled—or tossed in the air, as you might see through the window of your local pizza shop.

Because gluten is derived from wheat, people sometimes confuse the two. "Gluten free" and "wheat free" are often used on food packaging interchangeably, but they are not the same thing. People with wheat allergies have reactions to albumin and globulin, while people with gluten sensitivities have trouble processing gluten alone. Wheat allergies usually begin in infancy and last until age three or five, but some people remain allergic through adulthood. Those with wheat allergies can eat other grains (like barley, rye, and oats) that those with gluten sensitivities can't eat.

Barley, rye, and other cereal grains also have albumins, globulins, prolamins, and glutelins. In barely the prolamins are called hordeins, and in rye they are called secalins. They have a similar structure to wheat gliadins, and can affect people in similar ways when they are digested. So even though these grains don't technically produce gluten, it's common to include them in the gluten discussion. When people talk about "gluten-free" diets, they're really focusing on the proteins in wheat, barley, rye, and triticale, a cross between wheat and rye. Avenin, the prolamin in oats, is similar to gliadin. It can affect people with gluten sensitivities, but usually not to the same degree as barely and rye.

WHOLE-GRAIN HISTORIES

Humans have been eating wheat and other grains for thousands of years. Wheat is actually the product of three different types of grasses that are believed to have crossbred around 10000 BCE. The earliest harvest of wild grasses is thought to have occurred around 8800 BCE, somewhere in the vicinity of the Fertile Crescent—the region of the Middle East that curves from the Persian Gulf through present-day Iraq, Syria,

Lebanon, Jordan, Israel, and the Nile Valley of northern Egypt. Around 800 years later, people began growing wheat specifically to eat, and over the centuries, the practice carried to Greece, India, and Germany.

By 5000 BCE, people were cultivating spelt, a variety of wheat also known as dinkel or hulled wheat. It spread throughout central Europe and became a staple crop with the onset of the Bronze Age in 3000 BCE. Spelt was highly nutritious, containing a balance of protein, fiber, carbohydrates, and minerals, and in the medieval times of the 5th to 15th centuries, it was a key ingredient of bread. Around 1200, windmills were being used to grind grain into flour. This made the process quicker and more efficient, along with the introduction of new agricultural practices like crop rotation. Bread-making became a serious business enterprise to feed a growing population.

THE WHEAT REMAINS THE SAME

Not every scientist is convinced that modern wheat is any different from the stuff our ancestors ate. In 2015, researchers in Canada grew seeds of 37 varieties of wheat that represented grains from the 1860s onward. When they harvested the plants and compared their nutritional contents to today's Canada Western Red Spring wheat, they found little evidence that modern wheat had changed. Their findings called into question the whole idea that modern wheat is responsible for gluten-related disorders, obesity, and other health conditions.

Another scientist from the U.S. Department of Agriculture compared the gluten levels of wheat from the early part of the 20th century with those of modern varieties and found no significant difference. While these scientists acknowledge the rise of gluten-related disorders, they point to things like overconsumption of wheat, changes in people's immune systems, and the widespread use of gluten in food as possible causes, rather than mutations in wheat itself.

A traditional grain windmill in Brittany, France. The wind turns the blades, which turn a millstone that grinds the grain into flour.

The Age of Discovery from the 15th to 18th century brought wheat from the "Old World" of Europe to the "New World" of North and South America. But it was the Industrial Revolution that really sped things along. Farming improved with the invention of new technologies like Jethro Tull's mechanical seed drill. Farmers could grow more crops—including wheat—faster and in greater amounts than ever before. People began moving from rural to urban areas. To meet the needs of the rapidly expanding population, millers began looking for quicker ways to produce flour in bulk. They also wanted to prevent spoilage, since the oil contained in the wheat germ would start to turn rancid after six months and affect the taste and color of the flour.

MODERN MILLING AND BEYOND

The solution they came up with would change the process of grain production forever—but, some would argue, not necessarily for the better. Instead of grinding the entire wheat kernel by stone, as had been done for centuries, millers began using steel or

White bread is less nutritious than whole wheat or rye bread. Some have blamed the popularity of white bread for a growing gluten intolerance.

▼▼▼▼▼▼▼▼▼▼▼▼▼▼▼▼▼▼▼▼▼▼▼▼▼▼▼▼▼▼▼▼▼▼▼

A LAB ON THE RISE

The Washington State University Bread Lab in Mount Vernon, Washington, is a research laboratory devoted exclusively to bread. The lab studies what grains to use; how to cultivate, harvest, and mill them; and the best methods of baking, brewing, and distilling. It examines the nutritional values of various grains, as well as things like flavor and texture. Researchers and bakers use only the natural gluten produced by kneading the flour and water. One of the lab's key missions is showing how bleached flours with all sorts of additives can be bad for health, and should therefore be replaced with affordable, nutritious alternatives.

▲▲▲▲▲▲▲▲▲▲▲▲▲▲▲▲▲▲▲▲▲▲▲▲▲▲▲▲▲▲▲▲▲▲▲

porcelain rollers in 1870. It sounds like a simple enough change, but the new technology allowed millers to "strip" the grain of both the outer bran and germ layer, leaving only the purest, whitest endosperm behind. This removed the oil and made the flour last longer, so it could be shipped greater distances and be available to more people.

The problem was, the germ and the bran contained the bulk of the nutrients within the grain, such as vitamin B, as well as healthy fiber, proteins, and lipids. But customers didn't care. Before rollers, removing bran and germ was a time-consuming process that drove up the cost of "white" flour. It became associated with wealth and prestige. The new technology made the flour accessible to everyone, and people were happy to be able to afford a "luxury" item—even if it was less healthful than the whole wheat, rye, and barley flours of old.

Another major change to wheat was the rise of industrial farming in the 20th century. The introduction of pesticides, artificial fertilizers, and crossbreeding programs (where different types of wheat or other plant are combined into a new variety) have fundamentally altered the nature of wheat. These practices began with good intentions: scientists hoped to end world hunger by increasing crop yields and making more durable plants. Unfortunately, as occurred with roller technology, these new developments had unforeseen consequences. Crossbreeding and genetic mutations—changes in the plant's

FOR YOUR ENRICHMENT

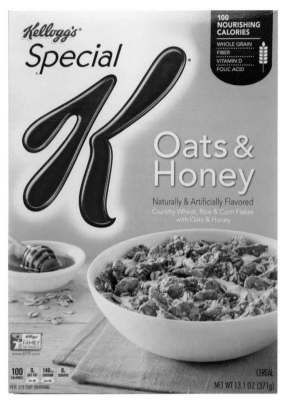

While many nutrients are stripped off the wheat in the modern milling process, companies do try to replace at least some of them by "enriching" the flour. This means adding nutrients that have been lost during production, such as iron, B vitamins, and sometimes calcium. Since 1998, the U.S. government has required that all flour be enriched with folic acid, a B vitamin that helps prevent certain birth defects.

The nutrient called folic acid is added to breads and cereals to help prevent certain health problems in newborn babies.

essential structure as it responds to toxins—have made modern wheat shorter, less nutritious, and far removed from the grain we'd been consuming for thousands of years.

Some nutritionists believe that these agricultural practices have changed the gluten structure in wheat and even increased its protein and gluten content, though this is debatable. Combined with modern baking methods like quick-rise yeasts that increase the potency of gluten in bread and additives like "vital wheat gluten" that make bread more elastic, it may be that our industrial-strength food-production methods are at least partially responsible for the rise in gluten intolerance over the last half century.

As scientists debate the pros and cons of gluten and the origins of gluten-related illnesses, one thing is certain: consumers and farmers alike want the healthiest, most robust wheat possible. This may mean breeding traditional wheat varieties that are no longer grown with modern varieties, finding alternatives to herbicides and synthetic fertilizers, and studying how the soils and climates of different regions affect grain production. By using the latest genetic-analysis technology, scientists can isolate the traits in older varieties of wheat that may be of use to today's growers. Some researchers would simply like to start growing ancient wheat varieties again, such as spelt, emmer, and einkorn.

Whatever the future holds, wheat is expected to be the world's most widely cultivated crop for some time. With a global population of 7 billion and counting, a key challenge for the future is how to keep people healthy and fed while making sure the planet doesn't suffer.

Text-Dependent Questions

1. What are the two main components of gluten, and how do they differ?
2. Is there a difference between "gluten free" and "wheat free"? If so, what is it?
3. What invention changed the way flour was milled in the 20th century?

Research Project

Research a gluten-free grain such as amaranth, quinoa, or buckwheat (kasha). Find out the places it is grown, cultures where it is consumed, and common recipes. If possible, prepare a recipe using one of these alternative grains. Write a brief report summarizing your findings and how you thought the grain tasted.

MANUFACTURE AND USE

Words to Understand

extraction: in gluten production, the process of separating gluten from starch.

glucose: a simple sugar that is an important source of energy for many life forms.

polypeptide: a chain of amino acids, which are the building blocks of protein.

seitan: a product made from cooked wheat gluten that is used as a meat substitute.

slurry: a thick mixture of water and some other substance that floats in it, such as particles of wheat flour.

starch: a white substance in plant tissue that stores energy.

Even with a little background on the chemistry of gluten and the history of wheat production, it can still be hard to conceive of what, exactly, gluten *is*. This is partly because the substance itself is so difficult to visualize. After all, it's not something we encounter very often in its raw state. A quick Google image search for "gluten" reveals tons of pictures of breads, baked goods, and different kinds of pizza, but almost none of gluten itself in its pure, rubbery form. You'll need to know a little more about the manufacture and uses of gluten to really understand it.

EXACTING EXTRACTION

As plants gather energy from the sun to grow, they produce a simple sugar called glucose. They convert extra glucose into starch, so they always have a ready source of energy. Starch is white, odorless, and tasteless, and it is an important form of energy for many living organisms. Foods with a lot of starch include potatoes, grains such as wheat, and corn.

The most basic way to make pure gluten is to mix flour and water and then remove the starch. The process of separating gluten from starch is known as extraction. On a small scale, this process is simple enough. Someone producing only a small amount of gluten at home needs only to knead wheat flour and water in a bowl, let the dough rest

In Japanese cuisine, fu is a form of dried wheat gluten.

OTHER WHEAT BY-PRODUCTS

 Gluten and starch aren't the only two wheat by-products sold on the marketplace. There are several more, each with its own health benefits. Here are a few:

- **Wheat bran.** This is the hard outer layer of the grain, which is removed during the milling process. It is high in fiber and often added to breads. People also sprinkle it on cereals or soups to help improve digestive health, lower cholesterol, and feel full longer. Wheat bran has many vitamins and minerals, including iron and potassium.

- **Wheat germ.** The germ is the part of the wheat that eventually grows into a new plant. It has many nutrients and is packed with protein. It can be added to almost any recipe to give crunch and texture, from smoothies to salads, and can substitute for breadcrumbs.

- **Wheat germ oil.** The oil extracted from the wheat germ, while hard to cook with because of its sensitivity to heat, can be used in salad dressings or sauces. It's very high in vitamins A, B, D, and E, and many people use it for skin and hair care. It takes a full ton of wheat germ to make one bottle of oil.

for a few hours, then knead the dough under running water to wash away the starch. This is done over a bowl so the person can see the change in the color of the water.

When the starch first rinses out of the dough, the water becomes milky. Gradually, as the starch depletes from the dough, the water turns clear. The person is left with a ball of dough about 20 percent of its original size and with a rubber-like texture. This is gluten in its purest form. Home cooks can use it for all sorts of things: as a meat substitute, a seasoning for sauce, or even baked or fried as a main dish in itself. Packed with protein and very low in fat, it is a popular choice for vegetarians.

While relying on the same principles, industrial gluten production is much more complicated and involves a lot of specialty equipment. In fact, there are several methods companies use to extract gluten from dough. The Martin process is the most basic. It is essentially the same as the small-batch, "home" production method described above, but done on a bigger scale.

In the Martin process, machines knead large amounts of dough, then send it into large, water-filled tanks. The dough is washed, separating the gluten from the milky, starchy liquid. After the gluten is recovered, the liquid is separated into its component parts, known as A-type (or primary) starch and B-type (or secondary) starch. A-type starch is used in food production, as a feedstock to produce ethanol (pure alcohol), or turned into glucose syrup and used as a sweetener. B-type starch is most often purchased by the paper industry to make cardboard or as an ingredient in glue.

One problem with the Martin process is that it uses a lot of water—about 15 parts of water for every 1 part of flour. It therefore generates excess wastewater. Also, all

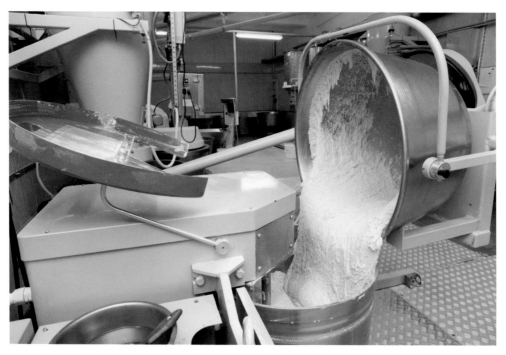

Bread dough at a factory.

that kneading can weaken the gluten and make it less nutritious. To fix some of these drawbacks, inventors came up with the batter or slurry process in 1944. A slurry is a mixture of liquid and free-floating particles—in this case, bits of flour suspended in water.

In this process, the slurry is stirred for several hours until the gluten begins to form. A screen is passed through the slurry to collect the gluten. The gluten is then washed to remove the remaining starch. Then the wet gluten is passed through a screw press to wring out the bulk of

EDUCATIONAL VIDEO

A CLOSER LOOK AT GLUTEN

Scan this code for a video about gluten and cooking.

the moisture, a step known as "dewatering." From here the gluten is fed into a drying chamber, where streams of hot air turn it into a powder-like substance with very low moisture. Gluten is very sensitive to heat and can lose its elasticity if it stays too long in high temperatures, so the drying time is carefully monitored. Once the powder is cooled and sifted, it is ready to be packaged. As in the Martin process, the A- and B-type starches are recovered, dried, and packed for resale.

Like any product, there are high-quality and low-quality glutens. The type of wheat the gluten was sourced from is a big factor, as some varieties have more polypeptides, or chains of amino acids, which are the building blocks of protein. During the growing season, too much rain, excessive heat, or an early frost can all damage the gluten forming within grain.

HOME AND INDUSTRIAL USE

Processed, powdered gluten is sold to consumers as "vital wheat gluten," a flour-like substance with many uses. Home bakers use it as a sort of "superfood," since just a small

HIDDEN GLUTEN

Medications and vitamin supplements sometimes contain gluten, as do some cosmetics, such as lip balm, lotion, and moisturizer. Even though people aren't eating these products, individuals with gluten sensitivities can still have problems if the gluten enters through the skin. Gluten is also used in pet foods and livestock feeds to increase protein content.

Gluten isn't just in food; it can be found in common beauty products, too.

amount will improve the elasticity, rising ability, and texture of breads and other baked goods. Many bakers add it to rye breads, since rye flour is lower in protein and benefits from a little boost in gluten. Vital wheat gluten can also act as a meat substitute or "extender" in recipes such as meatballs or meatloaf.

By manipulating the amount of gluten, bakers can get different effects in different breads. For instance, they might opt for a high-protein flour with more gluten when making a thick, hearty bread, or use low-protein flours with less gluten to make flaky pastries.

A very popular use for vital wheat gluten is to turn it into seitan, a meat substitute popular in Chinese and Southeast Asian cooking. Seitan is made by mixing the powdered gluten with water (or vegetable stock), spices, and soy or tamari sauce. After this mixture is kneaded into a ball and allowed to rest, it is cut into strips and placed in a simmering broth for 30 to 60 minutes. The resulting product has a chewy, meaty texture, and the additional spices give it a bold flavor. Seitan can also be baked, braised, or deep-fried. Some chefs experiment with different spice combinations to mimic the taste of sausage, chicken, and other types of meat. With zero fat and 7.5 grams of protein per ounce in its raw state, seitan is a healthy, inexpensive food option.

Industrial bakers add gluten to their products for the same reasons home bakers do: to give bread dough strength, improve its elasticity and ability to hold its shape, and enhance its flavor. When the yeast in the dough breaks down the sugars, it produces gas in the form of carbon dioxide. Gluten helps the dough retain this gas, so the bread can rise more evenly. Industrial-scale food producers use gluten in other products besides

Gluten can be made into a popular meat substitute called seitan.

Gluten is used in some salad dressings to give them a thicker consistency.

breads, such pasta and processed meats. Frozen battered foods, like fish sticks or chicken nuggets, get a sprinkling of gluten to help the crusty outside bind to the food.

Wheat is a huge part of most peoples' diets—whether they are conscious of it or not. In fact, nearly a third of all foods found in American supermarkets contain some element of wheat: either gluten, starch, or both. Most people associate gluten with "grainy" foods like breads and cereals, but it turns up in a surprising variety of products. It is used to thicken salad dressings and chocolate, added to some hot dogs and sausages as "modified food starch," and is found in wheat-based soy sauces. Even items labeled "wheat free" may contain traces of spelt, barley, and rye. All of these grains may affect people with gluten sensitivities in the same ways as wheat.

TEXT-DEPENDENT QUESTIONS

1. How does a person extract gluten at home?
2. What are the two processes for extracting gluten on a larger scale, and how are they different?
3. Why is gluten sometimes added to bread dough?

RESEARCH PROJECT

Check the ingredients of products in your family's kitchen and make a list of all those that contain gluten. Research at least three of these products to find out how they are produced, at what stage the gluten is added, and why. Write a brief report summarizing your findings. Be sure to include whether any of the products surprised you.

MEDICAL CONCERNS

 ## WORDS TO UNDERSTAND

antibody: a protein in the blood that fights off substances the body thinks are dangerous.

autoimmune disease: a disease where the body cannot differentiate between its own tissues and foreign invaders like toxins or bacteria, and so it attacks itself.

biopsy: the process of removing living tissue from the body to examine it for disease.

celiac disease: a disorder in which a person's immune system reacts violently to gluten, causing damage to the small intestine.

endoscopy: a medical process in which a doctor examines the insides of a patient's body with a lighted, movable instrument called an endoscope.

gastrointestinal disorder: an illness involving the digestive system.

non-celiac gluten sensitivity: when a person has difficulty digesting gluten or experiences health issues when consuming gluten, but does not have celiac disease.

The number of people reporting wheat- or gluten-related health problems has risen dramatically in the 21st century. These problems can range from a mild case of **non-celiac gluten sensitivity** to a serious disorder known as **celiac disease**. The reason for the increase in gluten-related complaints is not clear. Some scientists think it's the fact that we consume more gluten than people used to. This happens because it's now added to all sorts of food products, from breads to baked beans. Others blame an increase in overall wheat consumption, which has occurred as the technology for breeding and harvesting wheat has improved. Still others point to factors like genetics, the environment, or problems with digestion. Whatever the case, it's unlikely that we'll reach a consensus any time soon.

Celiac Disease: An Overview

Celiac disease is an **autoimmune disease**, meaning it is a condition where the body can't tell the difference between "outside invaders," like infections or toxins, and certain types of healthy tissues. In the case of celiac disease, gluten triggers white blood cells to attack the lining of the small intestine. This can severely damage the villi, the hair-

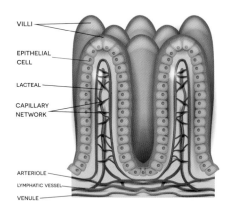
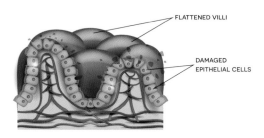

NORMAL VILLI   DAMAGED VILLI

Celiac disease damages the inside of the small intestine, impacting how the body digests and absorbs nutrients.

CELIAC FACTORS

Celiac symptoms are not always uniform. For example, some can be stronger or weaker, depending on the person. Some people develop symptoms later in life, after years of eating gluten, while others get them at a very young age. There are several reasons for this, including

- how long someone was breastfed as a baby,
- how old a person was when he or she started eating gluten,
- the overall amount of gluten a person eats, and
- how much the intestine has been damaged before celiac disease was diagnosed.

like projections that line the wall of the intestine and help the body absorb nutrients. Repeated celiac attacks leave the intestinal lining smooth, which prevents the body from getting all the nutrients it needs.

Celiac disease is very rare—only about 1 percent of the population has it. Several factors may contribute to developing the disorder. The first is genetics. If one of your parents has the disease, you have a 10 percent chance of having it, too. There are two specific genes that are linked directly to celiac disease, and about 40 percent of the population has one or both of them.

Another major factor is how much gluten you consume. Studies have shown that the more wheat and gluten we eat, the more cases of celiac disease occur. One famous study of the 1940s showed that celiac disease declined during the bread shortages of World War II and rose again after the war. More recent statistics show that cases of celiac disease have doubled every 15 years since 1974.

There are a few theories about why this might be. One is that the immune systems of people in industrialized countries have grown weak due to the overuse of antibiotics and vaccines, and that over-cleanliness has changed the makeup of good bacteria in the gut

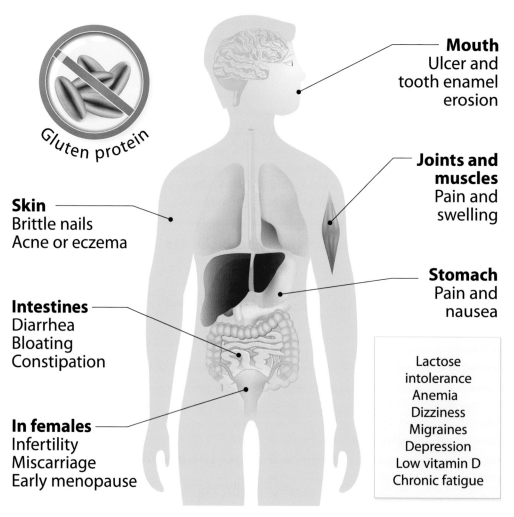

Mouth
Ulcer and
tooth enamel
erosion

**Joints and
muscles**
Pain and
swelling

Gluten protein

Skin
Brittle nails
Acne or eczema

Stomach
Pain and
nausea

Intestines
Diarrhea
Bloating
Constipation

Lactose
intolerance
Anemia
Dizziness
Migraines
Depression
Low vitamin D
Chronic fatigue

In females
Infertility
Miscarriage
Early menopause

Celiac disease can cause problems in a number of parts of the body.

that could help process gluten. Another theory is that children might be eating gluten at too young an age.

Other possible causes include environmental conditions such as infections, or "triggers" that can set off the disease. These could be anything from recurring health issues to stressful life situations, such as pregnancies, illnesses, or leaving home for college.

There are some 300 potential symptoms of celiac disease, and people experience them in different ways. This makes celiac disease very hard to diagnose. It is often mistaken for other gastrointestinal disorders, like lactose intolerance (an inability to digest dairy products) or irritable bowel syndrome. In adults, symptoms can range from digestive issues like diarrhea or bloating to mouth sores, skin rashes, and fatigue.

Because celiac prevents the body from absorbing necessary nutrients, it can lead to osteoporosis (weakened bones due to lack of calcium) or anemia (low red blood cell count due to lack of iron). More serious long-term problems include liver disease or intestinal cancer. Children and teenagers with celiac disease can experience growth problems or delays in puberty, as well as mental issues like depression and irritability.

Celiac Screening, Diagnosis, and Treatment

The first step in diagnosing celiac disease is to have a routine physical exam. If the patient's symptoms might be related to celiac disease, the blood is tested for antibodies.

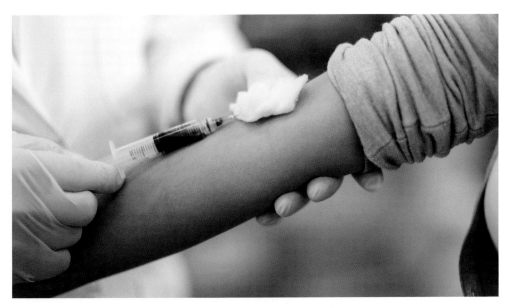

A diagnosis for celiac disease begins with a physical exam and a blood test.

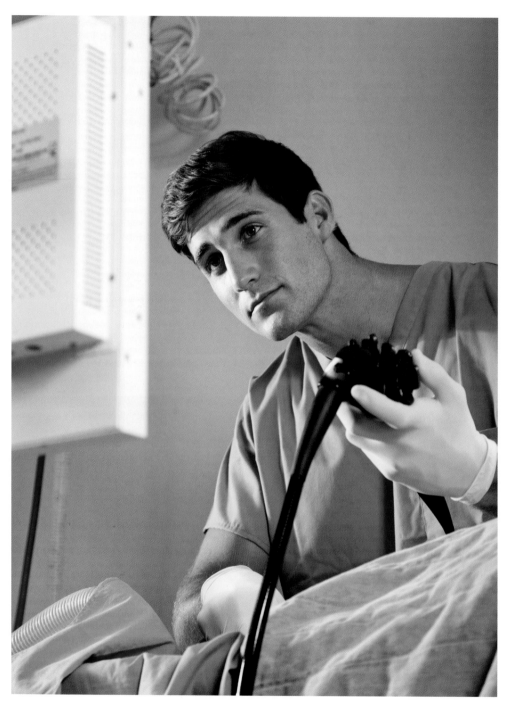

An endoscopy allows doctors to get a closer look at the digestive system.

These are proteins in the blood that attack substances the body perceives to be dangerous, like bacteria or viruses. In cases of celiac disease, a person's antibodies turn against a harmless substance—gluten— and cause damage to the intestine. People with celiac disease have higher levels of certain antibodies that can be detected with blood tests. The most common is the tTG-IgA test, which looks for tissue transglutaminase antibodies.

EDUCATIONAL VIDEO

LIVING WITH CELIAC DISEASE

Scan this code for a video about celiac disease.

If the tTG-IgA test comes back positive, which it does in 98 percent of patients with celiac disease, the doctor may double-check the results with other antibody blood tests. Another option is to do a genetic test to see if the patient has one or both of the genes associated with celiac disease. Since many celiac patients also suffer from a skin condition known as dermatitis herpetiformis (DH), a skin biopsy may be performed to confirm the diagnosis. Here, small pieces of skin tissue are examined under a microscope to look for celiac-related antibodies.

The skin biopsy may be enough, but the surest way to diagnose celiac is with an intestinal biopsy. In this process, known as an endoscopy, the doctor inserts a thin tube known as an endoscope through the patient's mouth, down the throat and stomach, and into the small intestine. The endoscope allows the doctor to examine the walls of the intestine for damage and then take a small sample of the intestinal tissue for analysis.

The only treatment for celiac disease is a strict gluten-free diet. Over time, the intestine will repair itself and the body will be able to absorb nutrients again. People with celiac have to be incredibly vigilant around all foods that have even a trace of gluten, from breadcrumbs to beer.

GLUTEN-FREE DIETS AND AUTISM

Autism is a developmental disorder that can make it difficult for a child to communicate and form relationships. Some parents of autistic children believe a special diet called the gluten-free/casein-free diet, or "GFCF diet," helps reduce symptoms. People following this diet avoid all foods containing gluten and casein, a type of protein found in milk and milk products like cheese. The diet is based on a theory that autistic children are highly sensitive to gluten and casein, and that they process these proteins differently than other people do, which increases the symptoms of autism. Another theory is that their brains react to these proteins as if they were foreign chemicals, which changes their behavior.

So far, there's no medical research to support the idea that kids with autism benefit from the GFCF diet. But some parents say they see improvements in their child's speech and behavior.

SENSITIVITIES AND ALLERGIES

Even if you test negative for celiac disease, your body still may react negatively to gluten. The standard term for this is *non-celiac gluten sensitivity*, or *gluten sensitivity* for short. Digestive issues are the most common symptoms, but so are a whole range of hard-to-diagnose problems, including chronic headaches, joint pain, and an odd, tingling numbness in the hands and feet.

Doctors are still learning about gluten sensitivity, and there are no foolproof tests for it. Some doctors may test saliva, stool, or blood samples, but the antibodies in these samples aren't specific enough to diagnose the condition. Instead, doctors rely on a process of elimination: they'll rule out celiac disease, wheat allergies, or other possible causes, then prescribe a gluten-free diet for the patient. If the patient improves, chances are he or she has a gluten sensitivity and will have to stay away from gluten.

A separate but related health issue is a wheat allergy, which is a rapid immune reaction to wheat. When a person with the allergy consumes wheat in any form, antibodies and special cells called *mast cells* are activated to alert the body that something is wrong. The mast cells send out chemical messengers that produce all kinds of reactions, including swelling of the lips and throat, a rapid drop in blood pressure, and severe itching. In serious cases, all of these symptoms might cause something called anaphylaxis—a rapid, life-threatening reaction where the person may experience difficulty breathing, nausea, and shock.

To test for a wheat allergy, a doctor will prick a patient's skin with a needle containing a tiny bit of wheat protein. If the skin turns red or bumpy, an allergy is likely present. The only surefire way of preventing an allergy attack is to stay away from all foods containing wheat. People with wheat allergies can still eat other grains, such as barley and rye. The condition is more common in children, and over half outgrow it by age 12.

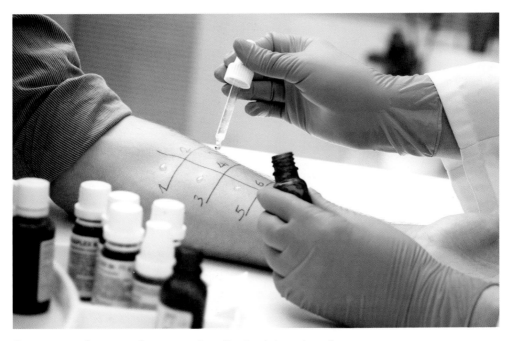

Doctors use a skin test to figure out what allergies their patients have.

FODMAPs

FODMAPs is an acronym for a group of carbohydrates with very complicated names: fermentable oligosaccharides, disaccharides, monosaccharides, and polyols. FODMAPs are found in all sorts of foods—not just wheat-based or other gluten-rich products—including fruits, vegetables, seeds, nuts, and dairy products like milk or ice cream. FODMAPs that are not properly digested pass into the large intestine, where bacteria work to break them down. This produces fermentation, which leads to all sorts of gastrointestinal issues, including cramping, bloating, and gas.

Recent studies have shown that FODMAPs may be responsible for many of the digestive problems associated with gluten sensitivity. The benefit of a FODMAP-

FODMAPs, other products known to cause serious digestive problems, can often be found in ice cream.

free diet is that it allows people the freedom to test different foods and get a more specific idea of which ones are causing problems. The diet allows for a wider range of possible food choices and is healthier overall than a gluten-free diet, which can be lacking in fiber, vitamins, and minerals. Because so many different types of foods contain FODMAPs, patients are advised to have a trained dietician help them eliminate FODMAPs from their diets.

TEXT-DEPENDENT QUESTIONS

1. What are some factors that might contribute to a person having celiac disease?
2. What methods do doctors use to test for celiac disease?
3. How does a person with a wheat allergy respond to eating wheat?

RESEARCH PROJECT

On your next trip to the supermarket or health food store, find a regular product and its gluten-free equivalent, like cookies, cereal, or crackers. Copy down the ingredients of each. What ingredients does the gluten-free version have that the regular version does not (and vice versa)? Research any ingredients you don't recognize. Write a brief report comparing the two sets of ingredients.

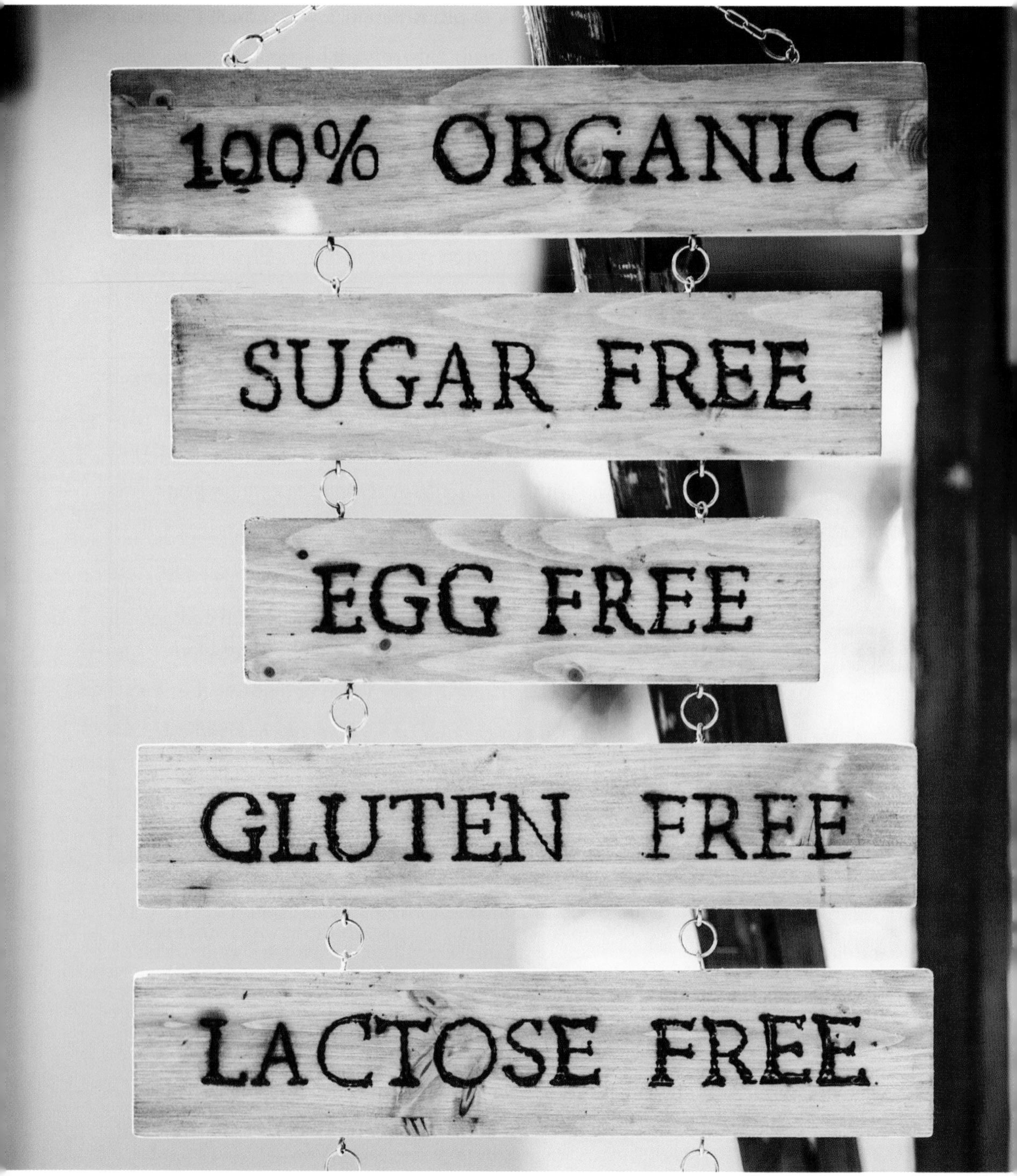
100% ORGANIC
SUGAR FREE
EGG FREE
GLUTEN FREE
LACTOSE FREE

GOING GLUTEN-FREE

Words to Understand

antioxidant: a substance that fights against the damaging effects of oxidants, which are molecules in the body that can contribute to heart disease and cancer.

cross-contamination: when a gluten-free food comes into contact with gluten, usually through the manufacturing process.

derivative: a product that is made from another source; for example, malt comes from barley, making it a barley derivative.

food additive: a product added to a food to improve flavor, appearance, nutritional value, or shelf life.

The rise of the gluten-free diet is an interesting phenomenon. On the one hand, there are more cases of gluten sensitivity being reported today than ever before. This increase may be linked to our increase in wheat and gluten consumption, cross-breeding programs, and genetic manipulation of wheat. On the other hand, the idea of going gluten-free has become such a cultural trend that many people adopt the diet even without any particular diagnosis. Thanks to all the publicity about the "evils" of gluten, some people decide they must have a gluten issue, too. More people are aware of gluten than ever before, and increasing numbers of people want to manage its place in their diets.

The Basics of Gluten-Free

A gluten-free diet is exactly what the name indicates: a diet that does not include the protein gluten. This means abstaining from any products that contain wheat, barley, rye, and triticale. Breads, pastas, pastries, crackers, and breakfast cereals are common "offenders," but there are lots more. By-products of grains with gluten, including malt (barley or another grain used in brewing or distilling) and brewer's

Gluten-free diets can be tricky because gluten can be found in a lot of foods that might not be obvious to you, such as anything battered and fried.

yeast (a yeast used in making bread and beer that comes into contact with grain), must be avoided, too.

A gluten-free diet is the only sure treatment for those with celiac disease or non-celiac gluten sensitivity. Since even the smallest amount of gluten can impact people suffering from these conditions, they must be aware of alternate varieties of wheat-based flours, like durum flour and graham flour, as well as wheat-based products like farina (the ground endosperm of wheat) and bulgur (kernels of wheat that have been cracked and precooked). Even certain food additives can be made from wheat and have gluten, disguised under names like "modified food starch," "dextrin," and "malt flavoring."

As if all this isn't enough to keep track of, gluten can make its way into gluten-free products through cross-contamination. This is when a gluten-free food comes into contact with gluten, usually through the manufacturing process. If equipment used to process wheat or barley is then used to process oats, the oats may become contaminated with gluten and unsafe for people with celiac disease or gluten sensitivity. Nuts and seeds are other products often processed in facilities alongside wheat. People on gluten-free diets may have to go so far as to call manufacturers to make sure a product is safe from cross-contamination, though companies usually add a "produced on shared equipment" label to the packaging.

Even simple home-cooking methods can invite cross-contamination. If you toast a slice of gluten-free bread after a slice of whole-wheat bread, the gluten-free slice can be contaminated. This goes for foods heated in toasters and convection ovens, too. People on gluten-free diets have to have separate sponges

EDUCATIONAL VIDEO

COOKING WITHOUT GLUTEN

Scan this code for a gluten-free cooking demonstration.

and rags for cleaning gluten-free utensils and kitchen surfaces, use different water to boil gluten-free and wheat-based pasta, and change oil when frying gluten-free foods to avoid cross-contamination. They also need separate cutting boards and jars of spreadable items like peanut butter, which can be exposed to gluten through utensils.

READING THE FINE PRINT

One of the keys to following a gluten-free diet is inspecting food labels very closely. Fortunately, many products are labeled gluten free to let consumers know they contain no wheat, barely, rye, or ingredients derived from these grains. In August 2013 the U.S. Food and Drug Administration (FDA) established rules for gluten-free labeling. According to the new FDA standards, any product labeled gluten-free must contain less than 20 parts per million (ppm) of gluten.

What does that mean, exactly? Well, "parts per million" describes how much of one thing is contained within another thing. Imagine a container holding one million seeds. If 999,999 of them are sunflower seeds and one is a pumpkin seed, the container has one part per million of pumpkin seeds. Scientists have determined that 20 ppm of gluten is the safety limit for gluten-free products. This is based on calculations showing that the average celiac or gluten-sensitive patient can tolerate 10 milligrams a day of gluten, or about one-eighth of a teaspoon of

HAVE NO GLUTEN, WILL TRAVEL

Those with severe gluten-related symptoms are often hesitant to travel. They're not sure if they'll be able to find gluten-free options when they are hundreds, or possibly thousands, of miles from home. Enter the gluten-free travel agent. These specialists set up trips for clients, calling ahead to hotels, cruise lines, or resorts to make sure they have plenty of gluten-free foods on hand.

People with gluten sensitivity need to choose their foods carefully; fortunately, gluten-free foods are often labeled as such.

GOING GLUTEN-FREE IN RESTAURANTS

For people on gluten-free diets, eating out can be challenging. If the restaurant has gluten-free options, great; if not, a person has to check over everything with the server: Are the spices and marinades prepared with gluten? Is the grill used to toast gluten-containing bread as well as meat? Are battered chicken fingers and onion rings fried in the same oil as gluten-free french fries? With the new awareness of gluten sensitivity in peoples' diets, many restaurants now offer gluten-free dishes on their menus. Some restaurants even specialize in gluten-free cooking, where patrons know that food won't be cross-contaminated.

Always talk to restaurant staff about possible gluten sensitivities.

flour. Spread this amount of flour out over 18 slices of gluten-free bread, and each slice would have 20 ppm of gluten. Someone with celiac or gluten sensitivity would have to eat *all* 18 slices in a day just to hit their 10-milligram limit.

It's a pretty detailed system, but consumers still have to do their fair share of the legwork. Producers of gluten-free foods aren't required to put the label on their products, though doing so helps customers and likely improves sales. They also don't have to test their products, but they do have to take full responsibility for calling something gluten-free. This involves careful storage procedures to make sure foods are kept away from wheat flour or other cross-contaminants.

Food manufacturers, in general, don't have to tell customers if there is gluten in their products; they only have to identify the eight major food allergens (milk, eggs, fish, crustacean shellfish, tree nuts, peanuts, soybeans, and wheat). Even if a product is labeled wheat-free, gluten can still be present in the form of barely and rye. Customers also have to beware of ingredients like "artificial flavoring" or "natural sweetener," which are often made from these grains.

APPROVED FOODS AND ALTERNATIVES

So, what *can* gluten-free dieters eat? Lots of things, as long as they don't contain—or come into contact with—wheat, barley, rye, triticale, or their derivatives. Meats, poultry, and fish are all OK, though they can't be breaded or fried in flour-based batters. Commercial marinades can also be a problem, since they sometimes contain malt, gluten, or other wheat-based additives for thickening and binding. If you're gluten-free, it's always best to make your own marinades with simple ingredients like olive oil or citrus juice.

Fruits and vegetables are fine for a gluten-free diet, as are most dairy products, including milk, cream, and cheese. Some people with severe celiac disease may have to watch out for blue cheeses, which may use rye-based bacterial cultures to get the unique flavor and blue veining. Nuts, beans, and seeds are great choices, provided

Quinoa is a popular and healthy grain that has no gluten.

they haven't come into contact with gluten during processing. It's best to buy these in their natural, unprocessed forms to be safe.

There are a lot of gluten-free starch and grain options, too, from staples like rice and corn to millet, quinoa, and teff (a tiny, nutty grain often used in Ethiopian cooking). And just because gluten-free dieters can't have wheat-based flour, this doesn't mean they have to give up baking entirely: substitute flours can be made from potato starch, garbanzo or fava beans, the seeds of the amaranth plant, and other sources. There's even a flour made from coconuts! Vegetable oils and distilled vinegars are naturally gluten-free, as are spices. People on gluten-free diets have to look out, though: some dried spice varieties can be cross-contaminated with gluten, and in rare instances companies may use wheat flour or starch to "stretch out" spices. Even in these cases, the amount of gluten is usually low enough (around 5 ppm in one recent test) not to cause any problems.

There is a whole separate market for products specifically designed for gluten-free dieters, from pastas to desserts to complete frozen dinners. Americans are projected to spend more than $15 billion on these products by 2016. They often cost much more than their "regular," gluten-containing versions: one marketing study showed that the average gluten-free customer spends $100 to fill up a shopping basket, while other customers spent about $33. Dieters seem undeterred by the cost, and supermarkets now reserve whole sections for gluten-free products. While it's good for people with celiac disease or gluten sensitivity to have gluten-free alternatives, there is a concern that many of these products are actually less healthful than the foods they are meant to replace. This is because manufacturers use refined carbohydrates like cornstarch to substitute for the flour they've removed, which takes away essential nutrients and fiber. They may also rely on extra sugars, fats, and chemicals to add flavor or improve the texture of foods.

There are many gluten-free products available; many are more expensive than their gluten-containing counterparts.

ALL-CLEAR ADDITIVES

 With all the additives gluten-free dieters have to worry about, it can give them some peace of mind to know that a few are clear for consumption. These include:

- **Caramel color.** This coloring agent is made from corn, not malt, as often believed.
- **Glucose syrup.** Though the name sounds like *gluten*, this ingredient is most often made from corn. If it happens to be made from wheat, it is so highly processed that any gluten is removed.
- **Maltodextrin.** Like glucose syrup, any gluten is processed right out of this starch-based additive.

Caramel coloring gives many sodas their appetizing shade.

Critics of gluten-free diets argue that a lot of the perceived benefits come from eating an overall healthy diet, rather than from the removal of gluten in particular.

ARGUMENTS AGAINST THE GLUTEN-FREE DIET

The questionable ingredients in processed gluten-free foods aren't the only concern scientists, doctors, and nutritionists have with the explosion in gluten-free dieting. One is that people are going on the diet without being properly diagnosed for celiac disease or gluten sensitivity. Some people think cutting gluten is a surefire way to lose weight, when in fact gluten-free products may lead to weight gain if they are not selected carefully. If people do shed pounds, it more likely has to do with eating more fruits and vegetables and less flour-based junk food like cookies and cakes.

Medical professionals are concerned that gluten-free is another in a long line of "fad diets" that promise miracle results but may actually make us less healthy.

A gluten-free diet lacks the valuable vitamins, minerals, and fiber found in whole grains. These grains also contain antioxidants that help fight cancer and heart disease. Gluten supports the growth of healthful bacteria in the gut, strengthening the immune system.

For the large percentage of people without celiac disease or gluten sensitivity, a gluten-free diet may not be the best choice. Instead of looking for quick fixes or miracle cures, it is much better to rely on tried-and-true dietary methods like portion control and eating a balance of fruits, vegetables, whole grains, and protein. If you feel you have problems digesting gluten, it's best to consult a doctor and get properly tested before making any drastic changes to your diet.

 ## TEXT-DEPENDENT QUESTIONS

1. What is cross-contamination, and why do people on gluten-free diets have to beware of it?
2. Why are some gluten-free products less healthful than the foods they are supposed to replace?
3. What are some arguments against the gluten-free diet for people without celiac disease or gluten sensitivity?

 ## RESEARCH PROJECT

Pay a visit to a restaurant in your local area. Ask a few questions about their gluten-free policy: Do they have gluten-free options? How often do they serve people who are gluten-free? Have they seen an increase in gluten-free customers over the years? Write a brief report about what you learned from the interview.

FURTHER READING

BOOKS AND ARTICLES

Celiac Disease Foundation. "What is Gluten?" https://celiac.org/live-gluten-free/glutenfreediet/what-is-gluten.

Green, Peter H.R., and Rory Jones. *Gluten Exposed: The Science Behind the Hype and How to Navigate to a Healthy, Sympton-Free Life.* New York: William Morrow, 2016.

Hertzberg, Jeff, and Zoë François. *Gluten-Free Artisan Bread in Five Minutes a Day: The Baking Revolution Continues with 90 New, Delicious, and Easy Recipes Made with Gluten-Free Flours.* New York: Thomas Dunne, 2014.

Jaret, Peter. "The Truth About Gluten." WebMD. http://www.webmd.com/diet/healthy-kitchen-11/truth-about-gluten.

Philpott, Tom. "The Real Problem with Bread (It's Probably Not Gluten)." *Mother Jones*, February 2015. http://www.motherjones.com/environment/2015/02/bread-gluten-rising-yeast-health-problem.

Rettner, Rachael. "Most People Shouldn't Eat Gluten-Free." *Scientific American*, March 11, 2013. http://www.scientificamerican.com/article/most-people-shouldnt-eat-gluten-free.

Rogosa, Eli. *Restoring Heritage Grains: The Culture, Biodiversity, Resilience, and Cuisine of Ancient Wheats.* White River Junction, VT: Chelsea Green, 2016.

Rubel, William. *Bread: A Global History.* London: Reaktion, 2011.

WEBSITES

Beyond Celiac

http://www.beyondceliac.org

A comprehensive website covering all aspects of celiac disease: living with it, finding gluten-free foods, and staying up-to-date on the latest news and information.

Gluten-Free Living

http://www.glutenfreeliving.com.

The online home of the magazine *Gluten-Free Living*.

U.S. Food and Drug Administration

http://www.fda.gov

For detailed information about allergens, gluten-free labeling, and any other topic related to public health, the website of the FDA is always a good place to start.

EDUCATIONAL VIDEOS

Chapter One: AsapScience. "What the Heck is Gluten?" https://www.youtube.com/watch?v=DXjpb7SFi3s.

Chapter Two: America's Test Kitchen. "Science: A Closer Look at Gluten." https://www.youtube.com/watch?v=zDEcvSc2UKA.

Chapter Three: LivingHealthyChicago. "Living with Celiac Disease." https://www.youtube.com/watch?v=vqvdKpDK0tE.

Chapter Four: Everyday Health. "Gluten-Free Pasta with Chickpea Flour." https://www.youtube.com/watch?v=5882SHf5cZ4.

SERIES GLOSSARY

amino acid: an organic molecule that is the building block of proteins.

antibody: a protein in the blood that fights off substances the body thinks are dangerous.

antioxidant: a substance that fights against free radicals, molecules in the body that can damage other cells.

biofortification: the process of improving the nutritional value of crops through breeding or genetic modification.

calories: units of energy.

caramelization: the process by which the natural sugars in foods brown when heated, creating a nutty flavor.

carbohydrates: starches, sugars, and fibers found in food; a main source of energy for the body.

carcinogen: something that causes cancer.

carnivorous: meat-eating.

cholesterol: a soft, waxy substance present in all parts of the body, including the skin, muscles, liver, and intestines.

collagen: a fibrous protein that makes up much of the body's connective tissues.

deficiency: a lack of something, such as a nutrient in one's diet.

derivative: a product that is made from another source; for example, malt comes from barley, making it a barley derivative.

diabetes: a disease in which the body's ability to produce the hormone insulin is impaired.

emulsifiers: chemicals that allow mixtures to blend.

enzyme: a protein that starts or accelerates an action or process within the body.

food additive: a product added to a food to improve flavor, appearance, nutritional value, or shelf life.

genetically modified organism (GMO): a plant or animal that has had its genetic material altered to create new characteristics.

growth hormone: a substance either naturally produced by the body or synthetically made that stimulates growth in animals or plants.

herbicide: a substance designed to kill unwanted plants, such as weeds.

ionizing radiation: a form of radiation that is used in agriculture; foods are exposed to X-rays or other sources of radiation to eliminate microorganisms and insects and make foods safer.

legume: a plant belonging to the pea family, with fruits or seeds that grow in pods.

macronutrients: nutrients required in large amounts for the health of living organisms, including proteins, fats, and carbohydrates.

malnutrition: a lack of nutrients in the diet, due to food inaccessibility, not consuming enough vitamins and minerals, and other factors.

marketing: the way companies advertise their products to consumers.

metabolism: the chemical process by which living cells produce energy.

micronutrients: nutrients required in very small amounts for the health of living organisms.

monoculture farming: the agricultural practice of growing a massive amount of a single crop, instead of smaller amounts of diverse crops.

nutritional profile: the nutritional makeup of given foods, including the balance of vitamins, minerals, proteins, fats, and other components.

obesity: a condition in which excess body fat has amassed to the point where it causes ill-health effects.

pasteurization: a process that kills microorganisms, making certain foods and drinks safer to consume.

pesticide: a substance designed to kill insects or other organisms that can cause damage to plants or animals.

processed food: food that has been refined before resale, often with additional fats, sugars, sodium, and other additives.

protein complementation: the dietary practice of combining different plant-based foods to get all of the essential amino acids.

refined: when referring to grains or flours, describing those that have been processed to remove elements of the whole grain.

savory: a spicy or salty quality in food.

subsidy: money given by the government to help industries and businesses stay competitive.

sustainable: a practice that can be successfully maintained over a long period of time.

vegan: a person who does not eat meat, poultry, fish, dairy, or other products sourced from animals.

vegetarian: a person who does not eat meat, poultry, or fish.

whole grain: grains that have been minimally processed and contain all three main parts of the grain—the bran, the germ, and the endosperm.

INDEX

ABOUT THE AUTHOR

Michael Centore is a writer and editor. He has helped produce many titles, including memoirs, cookbooks, and educational materials, for a variety of publishers. He has authored numerous books for Mason Crest, including titles in the Major Nations in a Global World and Drug Addiction and Recovery series. His work has appeared in the *Los Angeles Review of Books, Killing the Buddha, Mockingbird,* and other print- and web-based publications. He lives in Connecticut.

PHOTO CREDITS